Covers the ... updated

It's Another Ace Book from CGP

First we stick in questions about all the really important stuff you need to know about Solids, Liquids and separating them in Year Four Science.

Then we have a really good stab at making it funny — so you'll actually want to use it.

Simple as that.

CGP are just the best

The central aim of Coordination Group Publications is to produce top quality books that are carefully written, beautifully presented and marvellously funny — whilst always making sure they exactly cover the National Curriculum for each subject.

And then we supply them to as many people as we possibly can, as cheaply as we possibly can.

Buy our books — they're ace

Contents

Answers to the questions are on the back of the Pull-out Poster in the centre of the book.

Published by Coordination Group Publications Ltd.

Contributors:
Angela Billington BA (Hons), MPhil
Charley Darbishire BA (Hons)
Chris Dennett BSc (Hons)
Katherine Stewart BA (Hons)
Claire Thompson BSc
Tim Wakeling BA (Hons), GIMA
James Paul Wallis BEng (Hons)
Andrew Wright BA (Hons)

ISBN 1-84146-263-2
Groovy website: www.cgpbooks.co.uk
Jolly bits of clipart from CorelDRAW
Printed by Elanders Hindson, Newcastle upon Tyne.

1000

Solids and Liquids

Some things are solid and some things are liquid. This page is about telling them apart.

Q1 Say whether each of these objects is a solid or a liquid. I've done the first two for you.

Stone

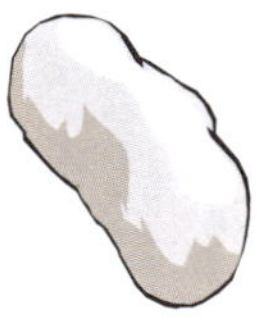

a) Solid

Coffee

b) Liquid

Wood

c) ....

Spade

d) ....

Water

e) ....

China plate

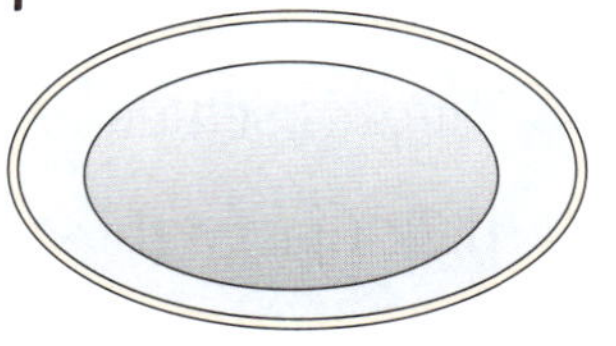

f) ....

Steel chisel

g) ....

Rhubarb juice

h) ....

Gold

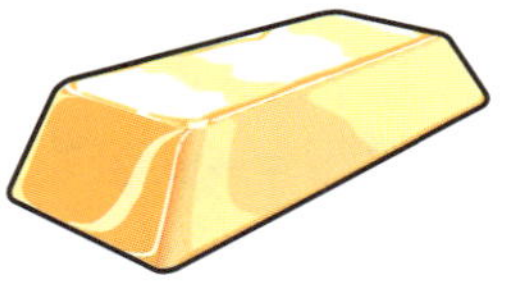

i) ....

Tomato sauce

j) ....

Oil

k) ....

Shampoo

l) ....

Ace shampoo — hair today, gone tomorrow.

Always start with a good SOLID first page...

There's loads of groovy stuff you have to know about liquids and solids — but I'll get onto all that on the next page. For now, just make sure you can tell solids from liquids. Piece of cake, really.

Solids and Liquids

There are lots of differences between solids and liquids. Solids are usually harder than liquids. Also, solids don't change shape as easily as liquids.

Q1 Put a tick next to the thing that Jimbob can pick up, and a cross next to the things that will run out of his hand.

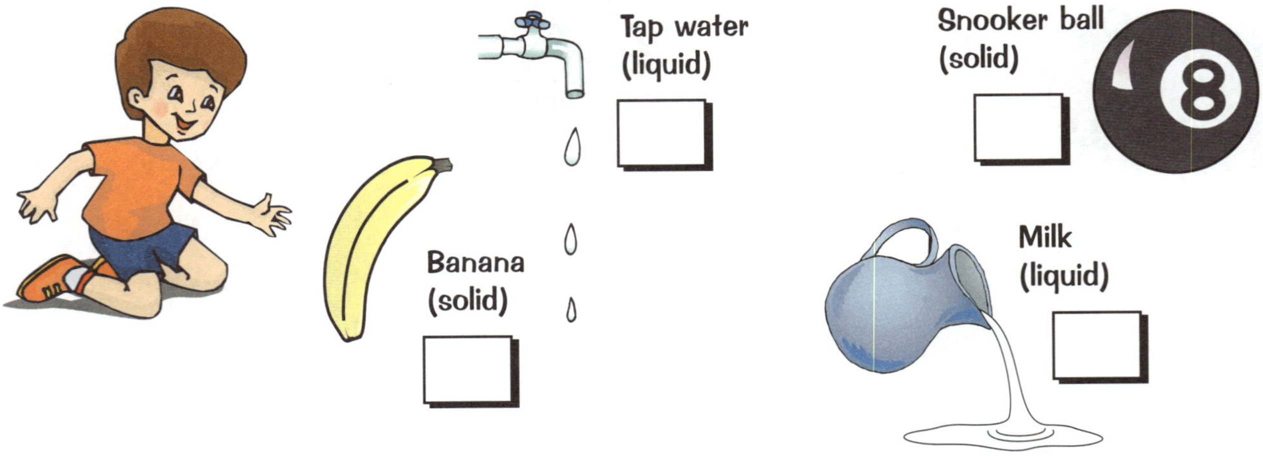

Complete this sentence by circling the right word in the brackets.

He can pick up the things that are (SOLID / LIQUID), but not those that are (SOLID / LIQUID).

Q2 Shelley wants to pour things into her bucket. That means they have to be runny. Tick the ones she can pour in. Then complete the sentences by circling the right word in the brackets.

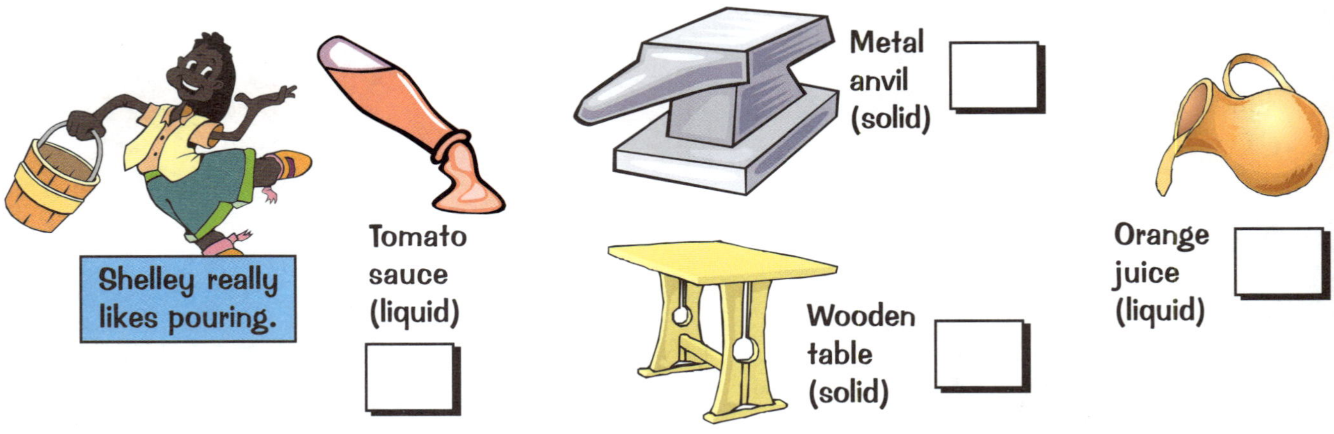

She can pour both of the things that are (SOLID / LIQUID), but not the things that are (SOLID / LIQUID). That means that a (SOLID / LIQUID) takes the shape of a container.

But a (SOLID / LIQUID) has a fixed shape — it doesn't take the shape of a container.

Liquids are cowards — always running away...

The two big differences between solids and liquids are: 1) you can hold solids but not liquids, and 2) you can pour liquids into any shaped container but solids usually stay the same shape.

Solids and Liquids

Not all liquids are the same. Some liquids are really runny, and some are thick and gloopy. But even liquids that aren't very runny are still liquids.

Q1 Put these liquids in order of runniness. Write "1" for the most runny, and "3" for the least.

....

It's not always easy to tell solids from liquids. Sometimes you really have to think about it.

Q2 Complete these sentences about solids and liquids by circling the right words.

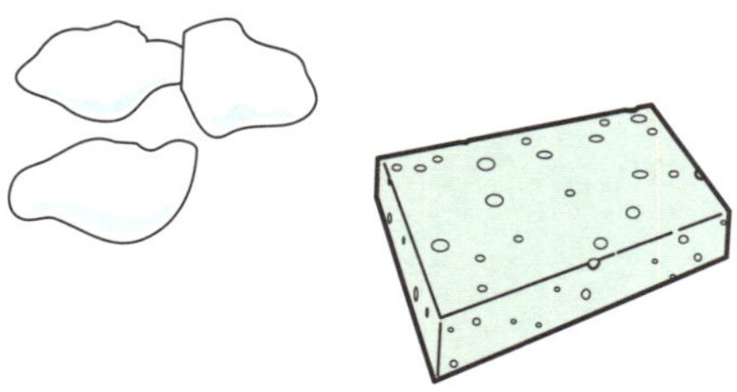

Cotton wool and sponges (CHANGE / KEEP) their shape easily. But they're still solids. They've just got lots of (RABBITS / AIR) inside them.

Rice and sand can be (TICKLED / POURED). But they're still solids. They're just made of loads and loads of (BIG / TINY) bits of solid.

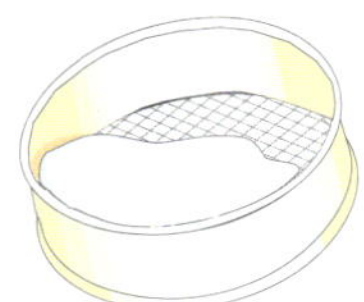

Q3 Name two liquids and two solids you can see on the table below.

Solid 1) ....

Solid 2) ....

Liquid 1) ....

Liquid 2) ....

A window's made of tiny bits — kick a ball at it and see...*

Phew — there's oodles of stuff for you to remember on this page. Liquids can be really runny, or not that runny at all. And sometimes solids can be squishy, or so small you can pour them.

**Don't do this. You'll be in serious trouble.*

Measuring Liquids

You can't just use a ruler to measure a liquid.
Liquids are runny, so you have to pour them into a measuring container to find the volume.

Q1 I bought a bottle of Ace Turnip Juice and wanted to find out how much was in it. I had three different shaped measuring containers, so I tried all of them.

First I poured it into a square tub...

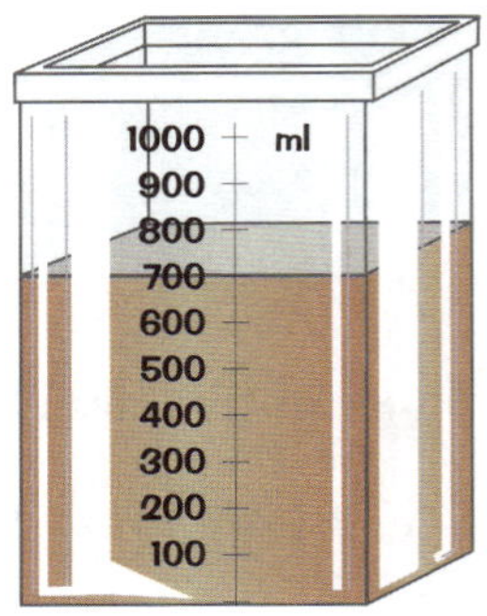

.... ml

... then into a round measuring cylinder...

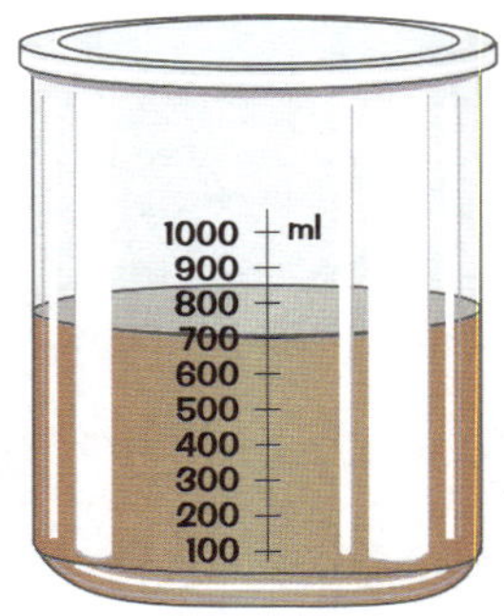

.... ml

... and finally I used a cone-shaped flask.

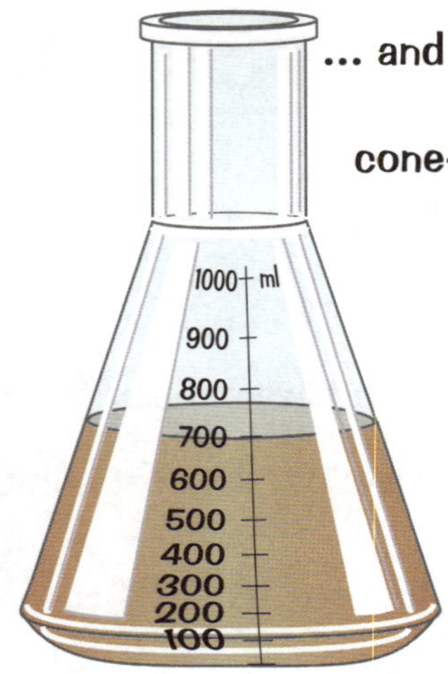

.... ml

a) Write the volume of Ace Turnip Juice underneath each container.

b) What do you notice about the shape of the Ace Turnip Juice when I pour it into:

the square container? ....

the round container? ....

the cone-shaped container? *It goes cone-shaped.*

I've done one for you.

c) Ring the shape the Turnip Juice will make if I pour it into this turnip-shaped jelly mould.

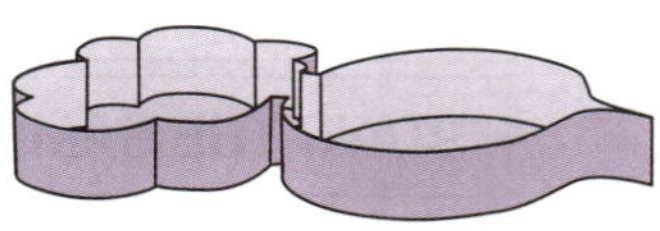

Cone-shaped Round Turnip-shaped Pear-shaped Square

I tried measuring liquid — but it ran away...

It's dead easy to work out how much liquid you've got. You chuck it in a measuring container, then read how far the liquid's up to... and that'll be the <u>volume</u> of the liquid. Simple as that.

More about Liquids

Wilma wants to pickle her toys. She needs these ingredients to make the pickling mixture:

1 litre of vinegar
100 ml of red gooey stuff
500 ml of Ace Turnip Juice

Q1 Wilma is using these three measuring bottles.

a) Draw the level of the liquid in each bottle, and colour in the liquid.

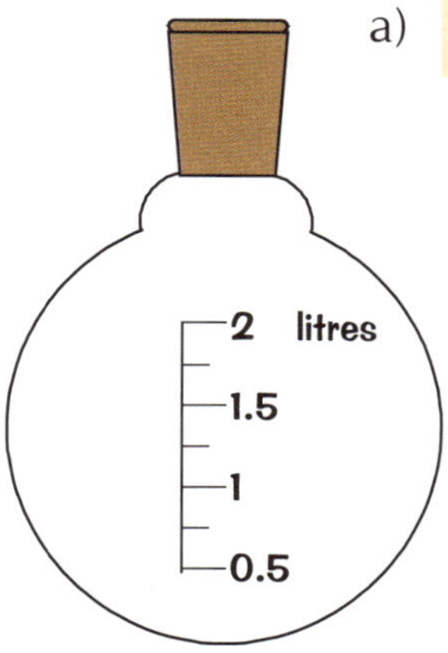

1 litre of VINEGAR

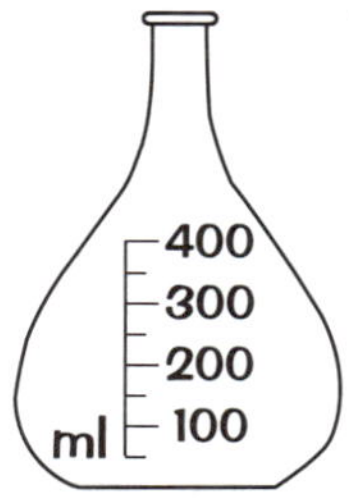

100 ml of RED GOO

Vinegar is brown and Ace Turnip Juice is yukky-orange.

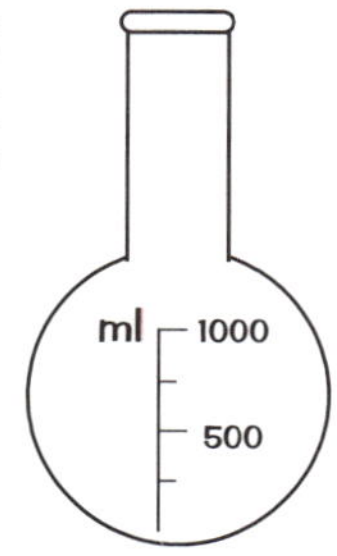

500 ml of TURNIP JUICE

b) Wilma now has 1600 ml of pickling mixture, and shares it evenly between these four jars.

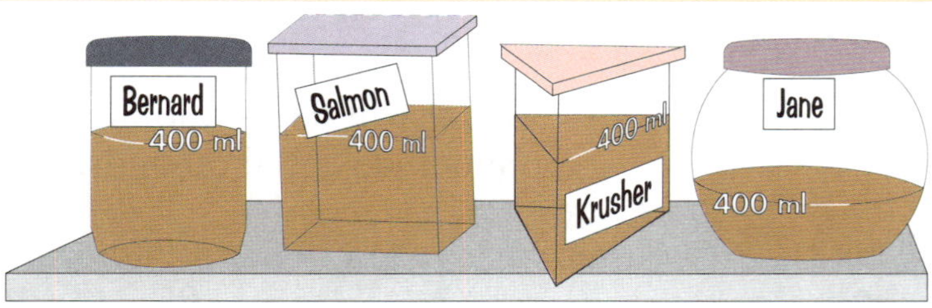

Finish off these sentences about Wilma's pickling jars, by choosing the right word in each box and writing it in the gap.

There is .... ml of pickling mixture in each of these jars. **40 / 400 / 4000**

The shape of the mixture is .... in each jar. **DIFFERENT / THE SAME**

c) This is a sentence about <u>all liquids</u>.
Fill in the missing words from the boxes.

If I pour liquid from one container into a different shaped container,

the shape .... , **STAYS THE SAME / CHANGES**

and the volume .... **STAYS THE SAME / CHANGES**

Don't change the volume — I like this song...

The liquid changes shape to fit the container — but it doesn't make a blind bit of difference what shape it is. If it says 400ml, it'll be 400ml whether it's tall and thin or short and fat.

Some Solids Act Like Liquids

Some solids behave like they're liquids — like sand, flour, salt and pepper.

You can pour them...

stir them...

... and they fall through nets.

Q1 When I tilt a tank of water, the water changes shape. Look at the pictures for these solids. Ring the one that will happen, then write whether or not it changes shape.

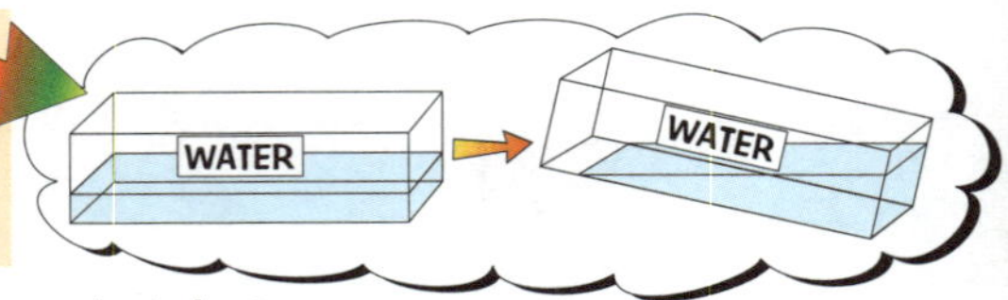

What happens to sugar?

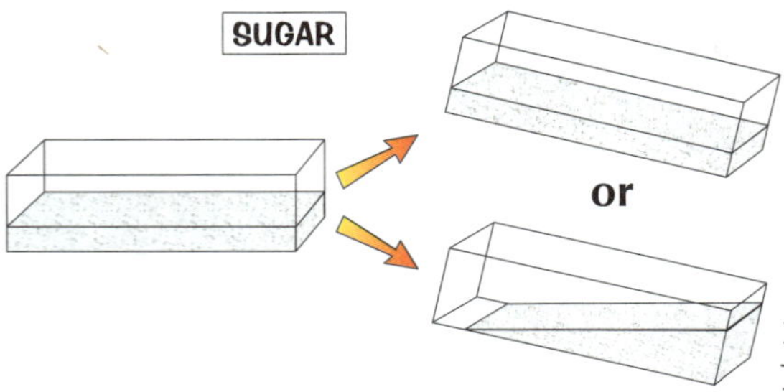

And what about bricks?

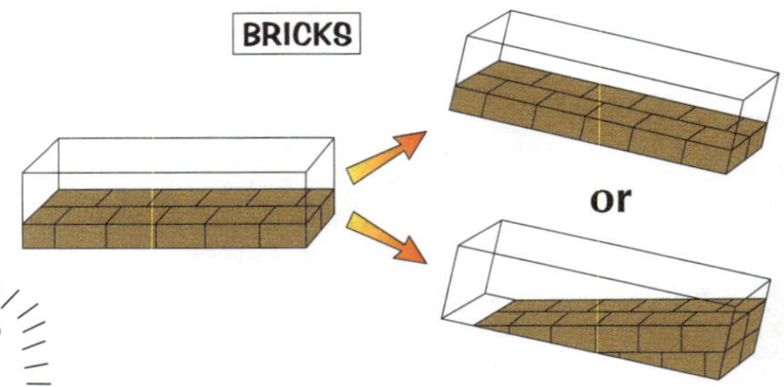

Write whether it changes shape or not.

....

Q2 For each of these questions, put a ring round the right answer.

a) Water goes through a net.
What will happen to a TV?

or

b) What will happen to these hundreds and thousands?

or

c) Water goes through a funnel.
What would happen to rice?

or

d) What would happen to a book?

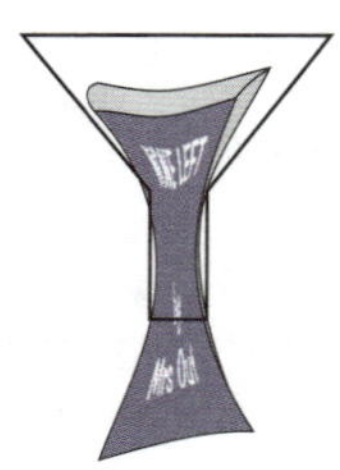

or

Nora threw a funnel.

Remember — just circle the answer.

Solids that flow — they cause a stir...

Remember that some solids can flow, even though they're not liquid. Weird but true.

Some Solids Act Like Liquids

Solids only act like liquids if they're made up of loads of tiny bits.

Sand is made up of really small grains. Because the grains aren't stuck together, you can pour sand over a water wheel and it turns.

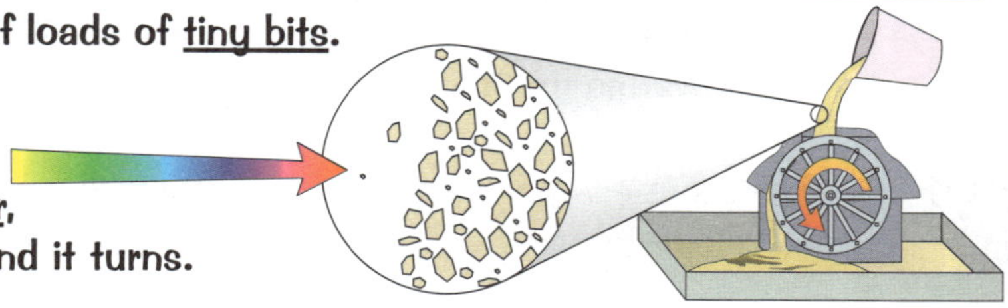

Q1 Look at all these solids. Decide which ones act like liquids and which act like normal solids.

Write "***Acts like a solid.***" next to the ones that act like a solid and "***Acts like a liquid.***" next to the ones that act like a liquid. Easy peasy.

a) 

....

....

b) 

....

....

c) 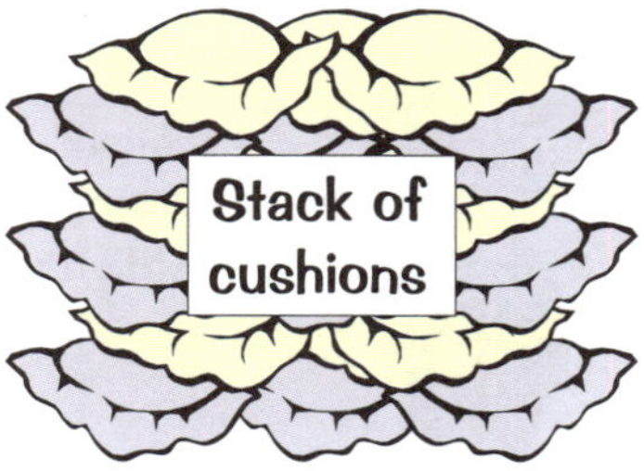

d) 

e) 

....

....

Q2 Find three more solids which act like liquids because they're made up of loads of little bits.

Don't use any of the solids on these two pages. That's cheating.

1) ....

2) ....

3) ....

Rex wished he could act like a liquid.

Don't get stuck — just go with the flow...

Rice, sugar and sand aren't one big solid but loads of little bits — that's why they flow like liquids. The little grains make all the difference. So it's not that mysterious after all... what a let down.

Water and Ice

When water gets really cold, it turns into ice — that's called freezing, or solidifying. When ice warms up, it turns back into liquid — that's called melting.

Q1 There's some water in each of these pictures. In two of them, it would freeze. Tick the ones where it would freeze.

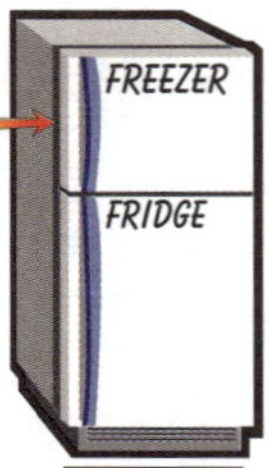

Kate's ice cream was just that bit too big.

Q2 The writing below tells you all about water freezing and ice melting. Circle the right word in each set of brackets.

When you have some water and you (cool / heat) it (down / up) a lot, it becomes (yellow / solid). It turns into (ice / stone). This is called (Henry / freezing / dissolving), or (melting / hardifying / solidifying).

If you have some ice and you (cool / heat) it (down / up), it turns into a (liquid / pumpkin / ice cream). When the ice turns into (water / a pumpkin), that's called (melting / solidifying).

Ice or water — yes, I saw water too...

One hugely important thing to learn here — but luckily it's dead easy. When you freeze water, you get ice, and when you melt ice, you get water. Ice and water are the same thing, really.

Melting Things

Water isn't the only thing that can melt. Loads of different things can, like chocolate or ice cream.

Q1 Circle the things in this picture that would be melting.

Q2 Here are some things that I don't want to melt. On the right are some ways of stopping things from melting. Match each object up with the best way of stopping it from melting, by drawing lines from one to the other.

Don't just stick everything in the freezer — some things don't need to be in there.

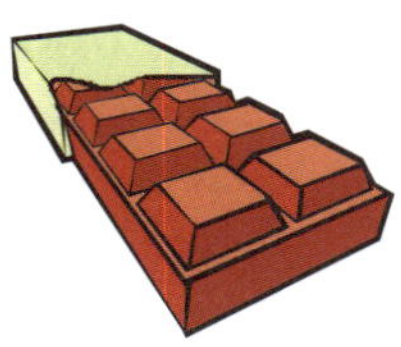

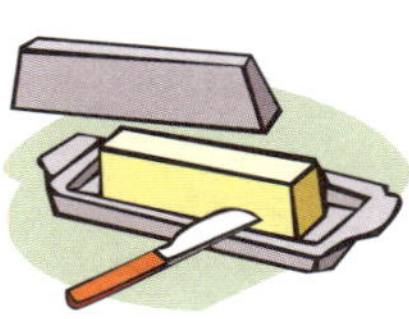

Keep it away from heaters and out of the sun — maybe in the fridge.

Keep it in the freezer.

Blow out the flame.

Keep it away from heaters and out of the sun — maybe in the fridge.

Leave it just about anywhere.

Keep it in the freezer.

She saw him and her heart melted — it was a chocolate one...

Melting isn't always bad. When you make a chocolate cake, you want to melt butter and chocolate. But generally you don't want your chocolate or ice-cream to melt in the sun.

Melting Metals

Even metals can be melted. You have to get them mind-blowingly hot, though. When they cool down, they go hard again. That's how loads of metal things are made into the right shape.

Q1 Here are some pictures showing metal being melted. Draw a line between each picture and the right words.

Melting metal so it can be poured into a mould.

Welding two metals together, by putting them together and heating them so hot they melt together into one piece.

Soldering wires together, by putting them together with a little bit of a soft metal that's easy to melt.

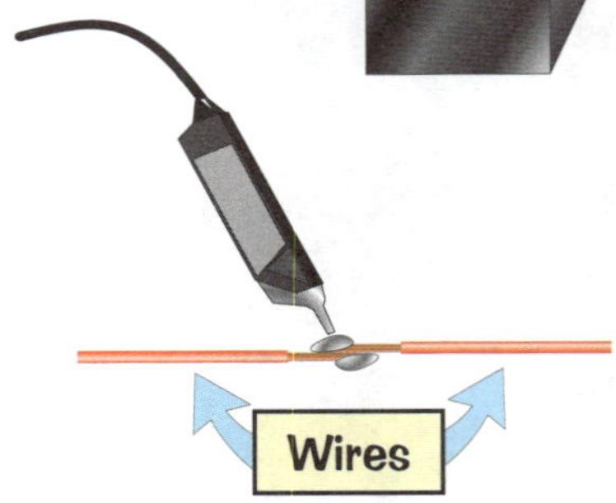

Q2 Write 'will melt' or 'won't melt' underneath each one of these pictures, to show whether the block of metal will or won't melt.

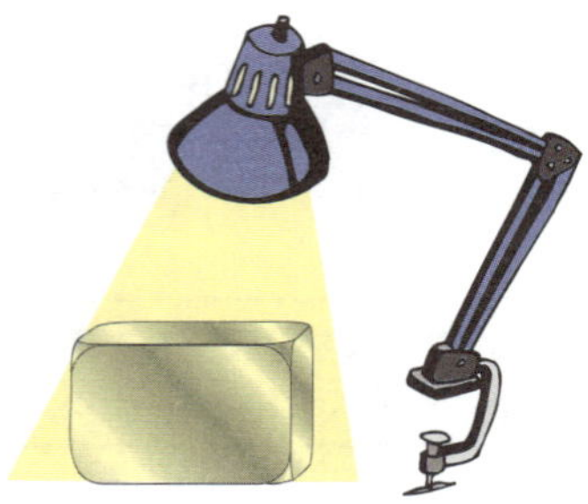

....

....

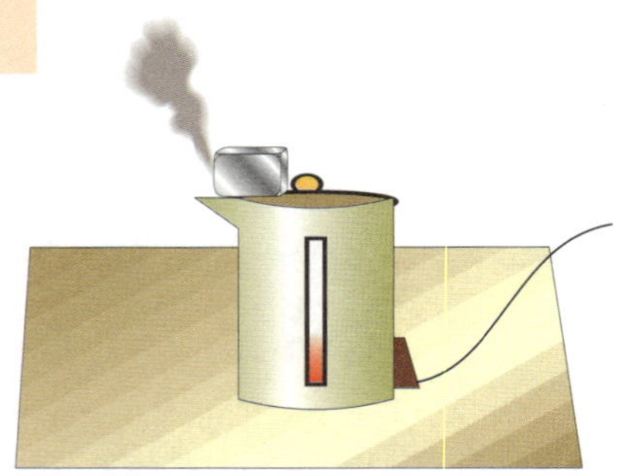

....

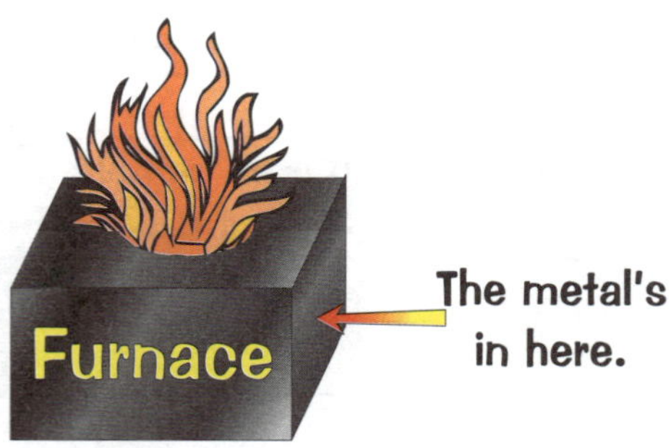

....

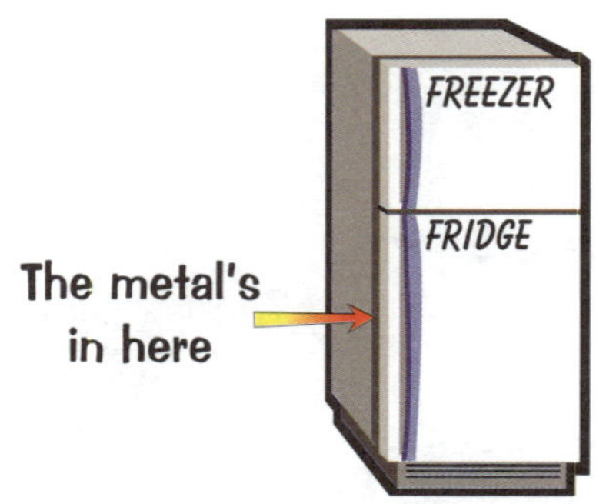

....

Phew that's hot — hotter than inside an oven...

Metals are really tough in the face of heat — they don't melt unless they're really mega-hot. That's just as well — imagine if your saucepans melted when you boiled an egg.

Volcanoes and Lava

Volcanoes are pretty exciting things. What I think is really great is that all that fiery red stuff coming out of them is melted rock, called lava. Rock has to be super-hot before it'll melt. When the liquid rock cools down it goes hard again, and you get new rocks.

Q1 Use some of the words in the blue box to fill in the gaps.

heavy, hot, cold, turns, lava, volcano, glowing, cools, moon, solid

Deep in the earth it's very hot. It's .... enough to melt stone. This liquid stone is called .... Sometimes the lava shoots out of the ground, from a .... Once it's out of the ground, the lava .... down, and turns back into .... stone.

Q2 Here's a picture of a volcano. Fill in the blanks by writing whether each bit of rock is solid or liquid.

To Gerald, volcano climbing was a way of life.

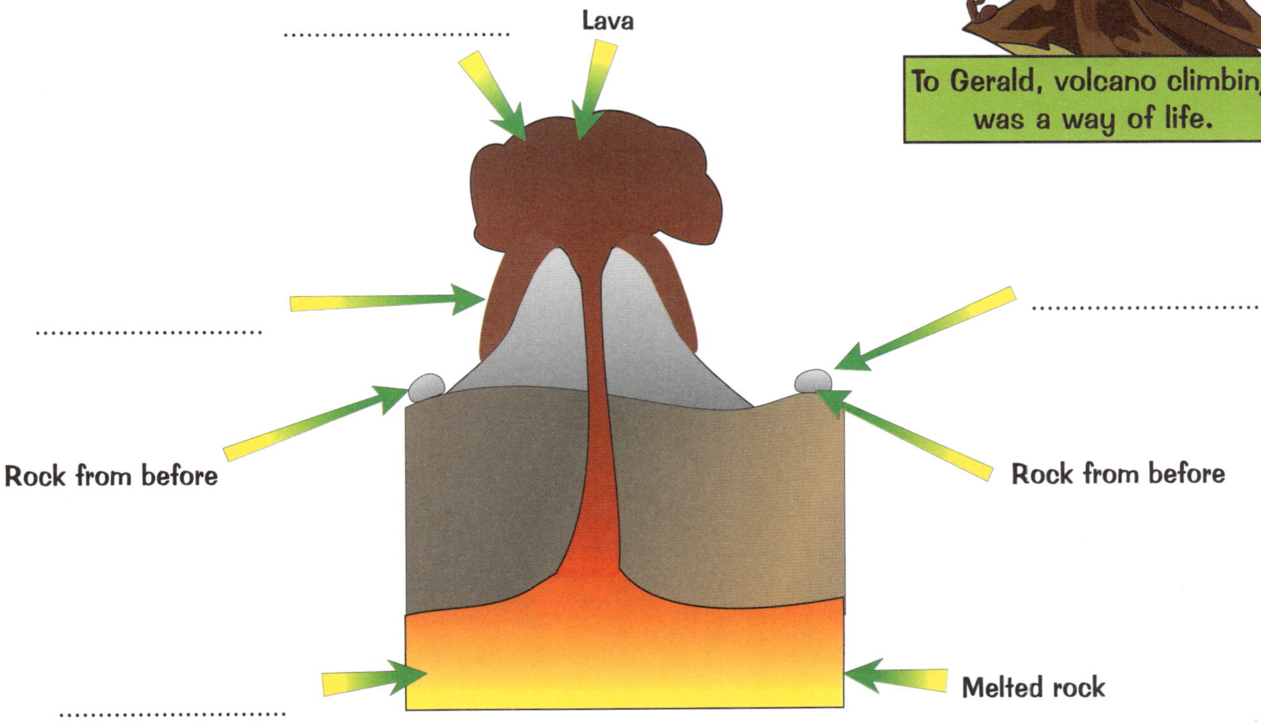

Volcanoes — don't blow it out of proportion...

Phew — it must get pretty hot if you're near a volcano when it erupts — when all the red gooey rock comes out of it. Volcanoes are great, but I wouldn't want to get too close.

Mixing and Separating Solids

You can mix different solids together — you mix flour and sugar when you bake a cake. But you can separate them, as long as they're made up of different sized bits.

Q1 Arnold has had an accident. He's mixed up his salt and his peas. He wants to separate them. Which of these four ways would be best?

.... ← Write the letter here.

A Put the solids in the sieve using the spoon. Shake it so all the peas fall out into the bowl.

B Pick the peas out with the spoon.

C Put the solids through the funnel using the spoon. Collect them in the bowl.

D Put the solids in the sieve using the spoon. Shake it so that all the salt falls out into the bowl.

Arnold gets mixed up in his bike...

Tick the things he'll need to use.

sieve ☐

bowl ☐

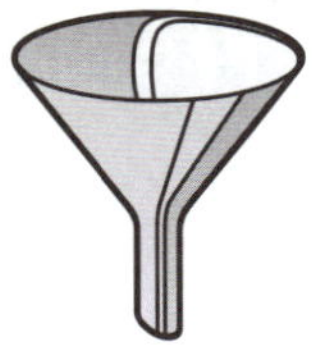

funnel ☐

spoon ☐

A sieve has lots of holes the same size in it. Only things smaller than the holes can fall through.

Q2 Fill in the gaps in the sentences below. Use the words in the blob.

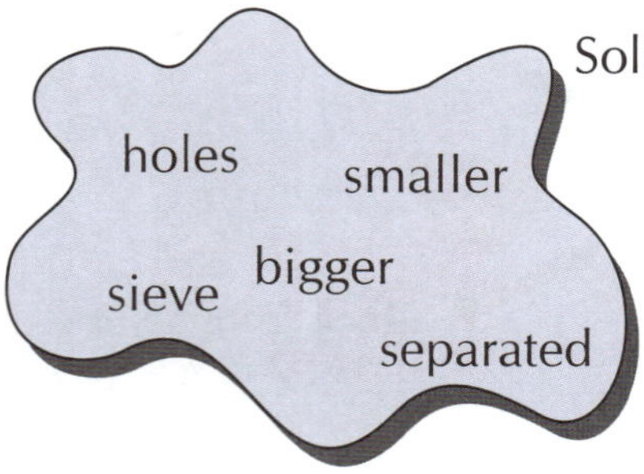

Solids can be mixed. The mixture can usually be ....

A good way to do this is to use a ....

A sieve has lots of .... which are the same size.

Anything .... than the holes stays in the sieve.

Anything .... than the holes falls out.

Separating solids — a book by Phil Terpaper...

Mixing and separating is important stuff. It's used for interesting things like panning for gold. They sieve out the stones first, before swilling the liquid around, looking for the gold.

KS2 Science Answers — Solids & Liquids

Page 13 Mixing and Separating Solids

Q1: Shovel, large-holed garden sieve, and bucket.

Q2: Bruce should spoon the rice and flour into the small-holed kitchen sieve, and stir through the mixture until all the flour has fallen into the bowl.

Page 14 Adding Solids to Water

Q1: Dissolves : salt / instant coffee / sugar / powder paint / flour.

Doesn't Dissolve : glass beads / rice / pebbles / sand.

Reacts ; baking soda / sherbet / plaster of Paris.

Q2: Accept any reasonable set of results.

Page 15 Adding Solids to Water

Q1: The wood chippings will not dissolve.

The gravy powder will dissolve.

The wax will not dissolve.

The Ping pong balls will not dissolve.

the washing powder will dissolve.

The fizzy bath salts will dissolve.

Q2: 1 : C 4 : F

2 : D 5 : A

3 : E 6 : B

Page 16 Separating Solids from Water

Q1: Stones and Marbles stayed in the sieve.

Water, sand & rice fell through the sieve.

Q2: Cross next to : sand / bird seed / chalk powder / peppercorns / sawdust.

Tick next to : cabbage / marbles / paper clips / small stones.

Page 17 Separating Solids from Water

Q1: The marbles are too big to go through the sieve, but the grains of sand are small enough to go through it.

Q2: Filter paper in a funnel would be best.

Q3: Filter paper has much finer holes than all the other objects. (Accept any similar correct answer).

Page 18 Separating Solids from Water

Q1: The best thing was the filter paper.

The second best thing was the small-holed sieve.

The third best thing was the large-holed sieve.

The worst thing was the fishing net.

Q2: Chalk powder — Filter paper.

Rice — Small-holed sieve.

Marbles — Large-holed sieve.

Page 19 Separating Solids from Water

Q1: holes / sand / smaller / filter paper.

Q2:

Page 20 Solids in Solutions

Q1: dissolves / solution / sugar / salt.

Q2: Sugar in tea , Powdered Coffee and Salt in Soup all can't be filtered out.

Page 21 Solids in Solutions

Q1: a) Sinbad could ladle his tears into the filter paper in the funnel and collect whatever came through in the pudding basin. (Accept any reasonable answer).

b) filter paper / pudding bowl / funnel / spoon

Q2: a) Tasting it.

b) Yes, there will be salt left in the water.

Page 22 Solids in Solutions

Q1: Use clean equipment. / Wash your hands. / Use fresh salt or sugar.

Q2: sieves / small / filter / big / salty.

Page 23 Solids in Solutions

Q1: a)

b)

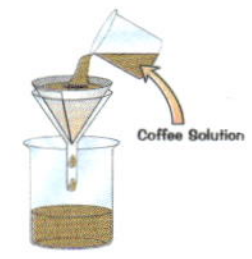

c)

(Accept any sensible diagrams.)

All answers should be 'stayed in the solution'.

Page 24 Revision Questions

Q1: Stool / Cannon / Wheel / Plate / Bottle / Ice.

Q2: Water, Tomato Sauce.

Q3: Water.

Q4:

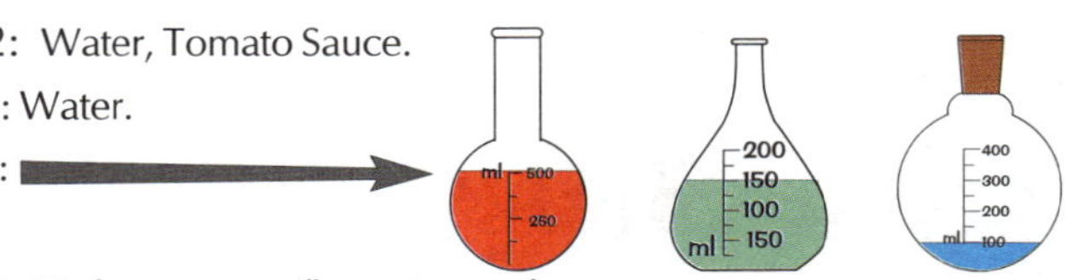

Q5: Ticks next to flour & sand.

Q6: Because they're made up of tiny little bits.

Page 25 Revision Questions

Q1: Small-holed sieve.

Q2: The holes in a fishing net are too big.

Q3: Large-holed sieve.

Q4: liquid / melting / cold / ice / freezing.

Q5: Rice & sand will not dissolve.

Sugar will dissolve & plaster of Paris will react.

Q6: No.

Q7: Yes.

VOLCANO
Coordination Group Publications
Really Important Stuff
The Revision Guide
CGP
Rock — SOLID
Ash — SOLID (powder)
Inside the Volcano

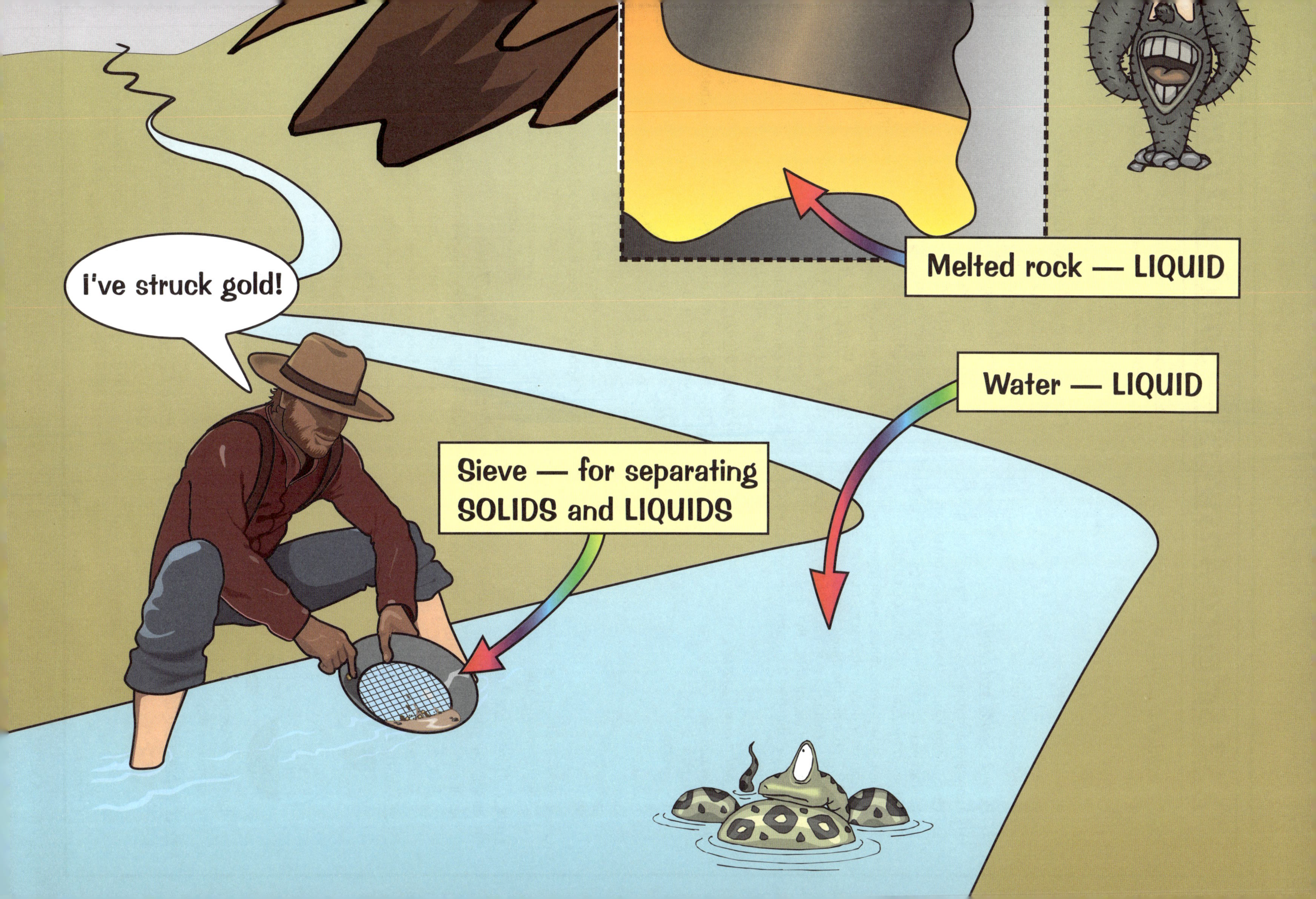
I've struck gold!
Melted rock — LIQUID
Water — LIQUID
Sieve — for separating SOLIDS and LIQUIDS

KS2 Science Answers — Solids & Liquids

Page 1 Solids and Liquids

Q1: a) solid g) solid
b) liquid h) liquid
c) solid i) solid
d) solid j) liquid
e) liquid k) liquid
f) solid l) liquid

Page 2 Solids and Liquids

Q1: Tap water and milk would run through his hands.
He could pick up a banana and a snooker ball.
He can pick up the things that are (SOLID / LIQUID), but not those that are (SOLID / LIQUID).

Q2: She can pour tomato sauce and orange juice.
She can pour both of the things that are (SOLID / LIQUID), but not the things that are (SOLID / LIQUID). That means that a (SOLID / LIQUID) takes the shape of a container. But a (SOLID / LIQUID) has a fixed shape — it doesn't take the shape of a container.

Page 3 Solids and Liquids

Q1: 1 — water
2 — soup
3 — treacle

Q2: change
air
poured
tiny

Q3: 2 solids from — plates / bowls / cutlery / chicken / peas.
2 liquids from — milk / cola / gravy.

Page 4 Measuring Liquids

Q1: a) 700 ml: 700 ml: 700 ml
b) It goes square in the square container.
It goes round in the round container.
c) Turnip-shaped.

Page 5 More about Liquids

Q1: a)

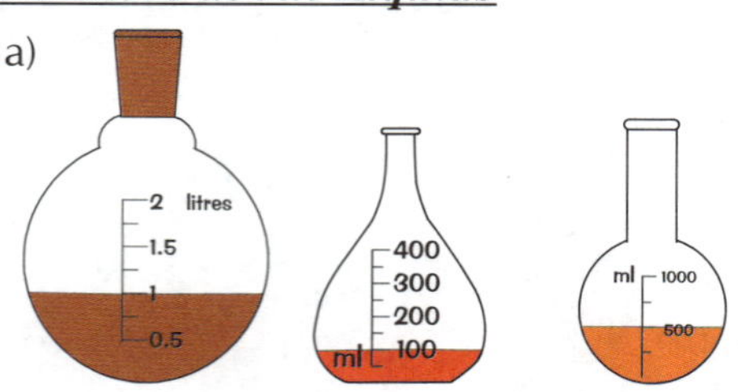

b) 400 : different.
c) changes : stays the same.

Page 6 Some Solids Act Like Liquids

Q1:

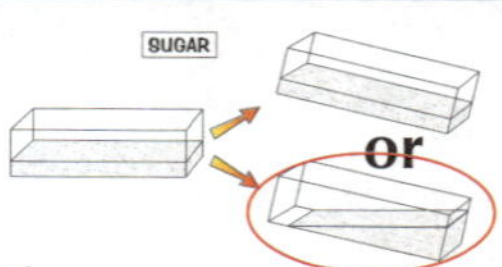

Changes.

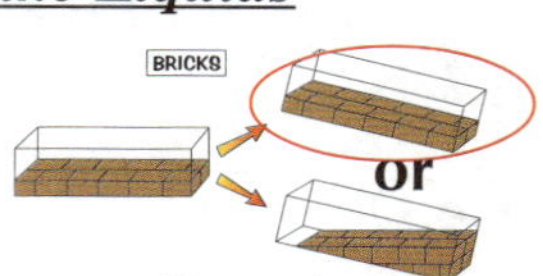

Doesn't change.

Q2: a) A television would not go through a net.
b) Hundreds and thousands would go through a net.
c) Rice would go through a funnel.
d) A book would not go through a funnel.

Page 7 Some Solids Act Like Liquids

Q1: a) Acts like a liquid.
b) Acts like a solid.
c) Acts like a solid.
d) Acts like a liquid.
e) Acts like a liquid.

Q2 : 1) Talcum Powder.
2) Sherbet.
3) Fine gravel.
} Or any other similar suitable examples.

Page 8 Water and Ice

Q1: The water would freeze in the freezer and in the snowman's hand.

Q2: cool / down / solid / ice / freezing / solidifying
heat / up / liquid / water / melting.

Page 9 Melting Things

Q1: The butter, the ice, the candelwax and the chocolate would all be melting.

Q2: Carrier bag — Leave it just about anywhere.
Candle — Blow out the flame.
Ice cream — Keep it in the freezer.
Ice cube — Keep it in the freezer.
Chocolate — Keep it away from heaters and out of the sun — maybe in the fridge.
Butter — Keep it away from heaters and out of the sun — maybe in the fridge.

Page 10 Melting Metals

Q1: The top picture — Shows melting metal.
The middle picture — Shows soldering wires together.
The bottom picture — Shows welding two metals.

Q2: Metal will melt in a furnace — it won't melt in any of the other pictures.

Page 11 Volcanos and Lava

Q1: hot / lava / volcano / cools / solid.

Q2:

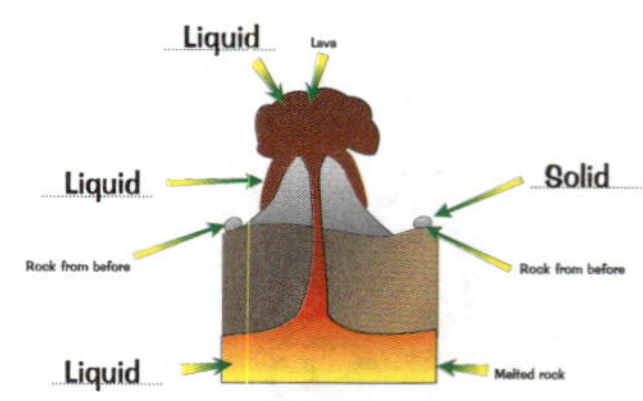

Page 12 Mixing and Separating Solids

Q1: D
He'll need to use a sieve, a spoon and a bowl.

Q2: Separated / sieve / holes / bigger / smaller.

Mixing and Separating Solids

You can get loads of different sieves. A kitchen sieve has small holes — so you can separate things like flour and raisins. A garden sieve has big holes, so you can separate things like sand and stones.

Q1 Elspeth wants to take out all the stones from the soil in her garden. Which three of these things should she use?

1) ....

2) ....

3) ....

Q2 Bruce is baking a kangaroo pie. But he's dropped a bag of rice into the flour. Tell Bruce what he should do to separate the rice and the flour, using any of the things at the bottom.

Bruce can use any of these things.

....

....

....

Getting rid of stones — roll them away...

This is actually useful stuff. Science that you might use at home. OK, you probably don't make kangaroo pies, but you might do some gardening and want to get rid of the stones.

Adding Solids to Water

When you put a solid in water, funny things can happen. It might dissolve so you can't see it. It might just sink and not dissolve at all. Or it might react — it could go hard or fizz.

Q1 Here's a list of solids. Which will dissolve, which won't, and which will react with the water? Write each solid under the right heading in the table.

salt plaster of Paris

glass beads instant coffee

sugar rice sand

powder paint baking soda

sherbet pebbles flour

Dissolves	Doesn't Dissolve	Reacts

Q2 Do this experiment (if you're allowed).

1) Choose five or six solids from Q1.
(Use some different solids if you don't have five of these.)

2) Put each solid in a beaker of water, stir it and see what happens.
Remember to use a fresh beaker of water for each solid.

3) Write your results in this table.

Be careful what you put plaster of Paris in — it won't come out again.

Put the sugar in the water...

Solid	Dissolves	Doesn't Dissolve	Reacts

Sounds like De-solving — is that like un-solving...

OK, so some solids dissolve, some just sit there, and some react by fizzing or going hard. You can find out what a solid will do by putting it in water. Fizzing ones are my favourite — they look best.

Adding Solids to Water

When a solid dissolves, it doesn't disappear.
You can't always see it, but it's still there, mixed in with the water — it's called a solution.

Q1 I want to know what will happen to each of these solids when I put them in water. My pet goat says they'll dissolve, not dissolve or react — but which does which?

Write here what will happen.

salt — *The salt will dissolve.*

wood chippings — ....

gravy powder — ....

wax — ....

ping pong balls — ....

washing powder — ....

fizzy bath salts — ....

Q2 I put some solids in beakers of water. Work out which solid I put in which beaker.

Write the letters here:

1. Chocolate powder ....
2. Salt ....
3. Chalk powder ....
4. Baking soda ....
5. Sand ....
6. Plaster ....

Hot chocolate — the solution to all your problems...

It's easy to tell if something's dissolved. Check whether all the solid has disappeared. If it has, then it's either dissolved or reacted. If it fizzed or went hard, then it reacted. Otherwise, it dissolved.

Separating Solids from Water

You can separate two different kinds of solids using a sieve. You can also use a sieve to separate a solid from a liquid (like water) — as long as the solid hasn't dissolved.

Q1 I got a large-holed garden sieve and put some water and some other things through it. Fill in the table to show which things you think fell through my sieve and which stayed in it.

Water

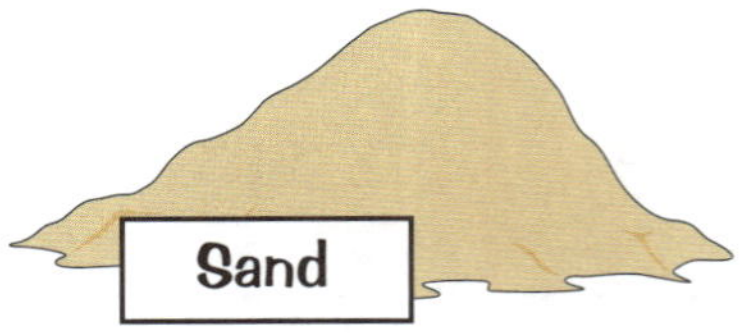
Sand

Stones

Marbles

Rice

Stays in the sieve	Falls through the sieve
....	....
....	....
....	....
....	....
....	....

Q2 Water always goes through a sieve — but some solids don't. I put each of these solids below in water. Now I want to separate them from the water using my garden sieve. Will I be able to? Put a tick ✔ next to the ones that will stay in the sieve and a cross ✘ next to the ones that will fall through the sieve with the water.

1) sand ☐ 2) cabbage ☐ 3) marbles ☐

4) bird seed ☐ 5) chalk powder ☐ 6) paper clips ☐

7) peppercorns ☐ 8) small stones ☐ 9) sawdust ☐

I've got a mind like a — what was it?

Sieves and nets are great for getting most things out of water. But they're completely useless if the solid can get through the holes — you're back to square 1. And you've got a wet sieve.

Separating Solids from Water

If a sieve is no good for separating a solid from water, there are other things you can use which will work.

Q1 Why does the sand fall through the sieve, but the marbles don't? Tick the right answer from the choices below.

- The sand is heavier than the marbles, so it falls through the sieve. ☐
- The marbles are too big to go through the sieve, but the grains of sand are small enough to go through it. ☐
- There are more marbles than grains of sand. ☐
- The sand is wetter than the marbles. ☐

Q2 You need to find something that will separate the sand from the water. Here are four things you could use. Put a tick ✔ in the box next to the one you think would be best.

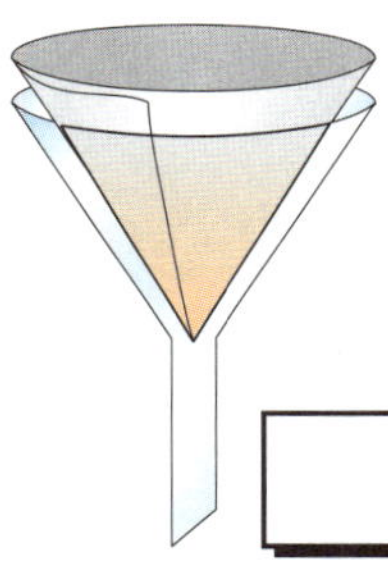

Filter paper in funnel ☐

Small-holed sieve ☐

Fishing net ☐

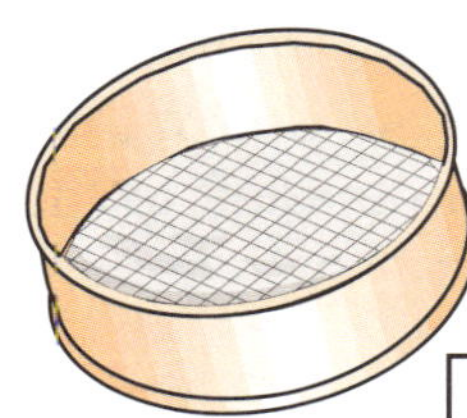

Large-holed sieve ☐

Q3 Give one reason why the object you chose is the right choice. Here's a clue — it's about the size of the holes.

....

....

....

Osmond the Viking has a mind like a sieve.

Learn the important stuff — filter out the rest...

There's one <u>huge glaringly important</u> thing, staring out at you from this page: It doesn't matter what you're separating or what you're using to do it... <u>it's the size of the holes that counts</u>.

Separating Solids from Water

If you want to separate sand from water, you need a kind of sieve that will let all the water through but none of the grains of sand.

Q1 I tried filtering some sand through various things, and I wrote down how much sand got through each time. Look at the results and put the objects in the order of how good they were.

Object	Small-holed sieve	Large-holed sieve	Fishing net	Filter paper
What happened	A little bit of sand got through	Quite a bit of sand got through	All the sand got through	No sand got through

The best thing was ....

The second best thing was ....

The third best thing was ....

The worst thing was ....

Suzy's pan wasn't the best for making pancakes...

Q2 On the left are three things I put in water. On the right are three things I might use if I wanted to take them out of the water. Draw a line from each object on the left to the one on the right that I should use.

Chalk powder

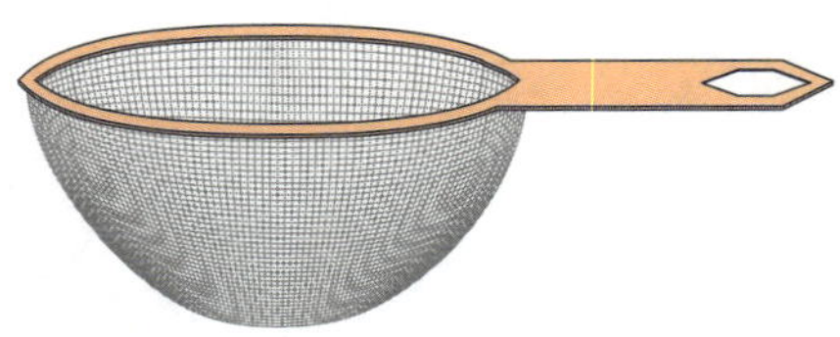

Small-holed sieve

Rice

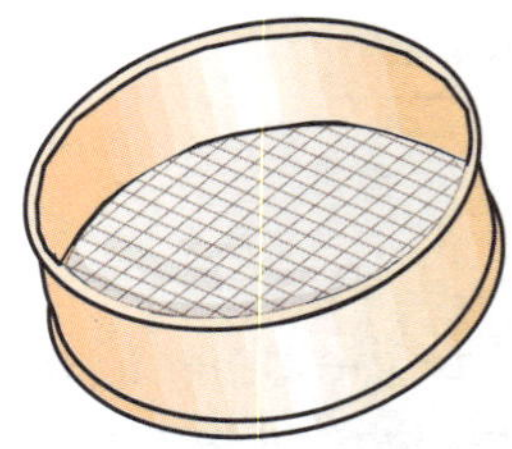

Large-holed sieve

Marbles

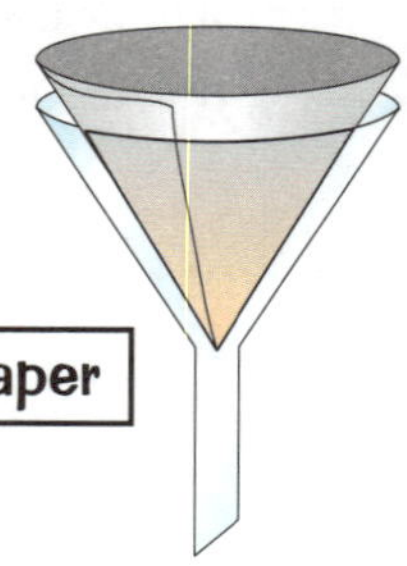

Filter paper

Getting rid of water — it really drains you...

Filter paper in a funnel is a pretty slick way of separating really small solids from water. You can be mighty sure when you use it, that the water will go through and the solid will stay in the paper.

Separating Solids from Water

You can separate things from water by using a sieve or filter paper.
The smaller the bits of what's in the water are, the smaller the holes in your sieve need to be.

Q1 These sentences are about a mixture of sand and water. Fill in the blanks using the words on the right.

A sieve has .... in it so that water can get through. Little bits, like grains of ...., may be .... than the holes and fall through. .... is like a sieve, but it lets water through and keeps the very small bits of sand.

holes | **filter paper** | **sand** | **smaller**

Q2 Read the clues and write the answers in the crossword — look back over the last four pages if you need help working out the answers.

ACROSS

1) You need to put the filter paper in this to do any filtering.
2) Bits of flour are too .... to stay in a large-holed sieve.
3) You use filter .... to get water and sand apart.
6) You can use this to separate rice and water.

DOWN

1) This paper lets water through, but not chalk powder.
2) Another word for getting two things apart.
4) A sieve has these in it.
5) This liquid goes through sieves.

Filtering — everything suddenly becomes clear...

All you've got to remember is that filtering separates a solid from water. OK, it won't work if the solid has dissolved or reacted with the water. But if it hasn't, filtering's a real winner.

Solids in Solutions

When you add sugar to tea it doesn't disappear, even though you can't see or feel it. It's dissolved in the liquid — the solid and liquid have turned into a solution.

Q1 Fill in the gaps in these sentences about solids and solutions. Use these words:

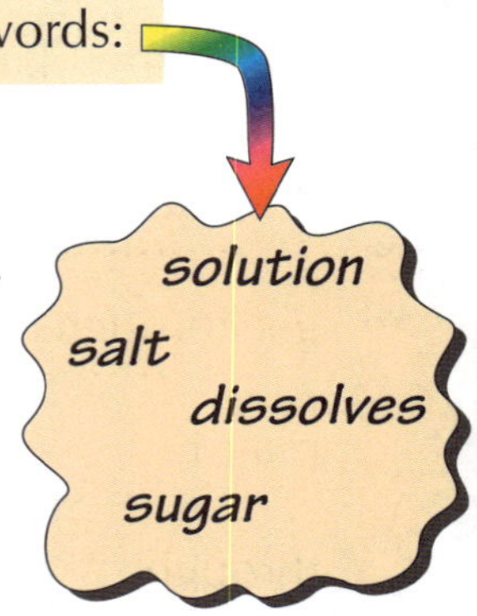

When you add salt to a glass of water and stir, it seems to disappear.

What really happens is that the salt .... in the water.

When this happens, you've made a ....

Some examples of solutions are .... in your tea,

and .... in your soup.

Salty water is a solution — which means you can't filter out the salt. That's because even the very small holes in the filter paper are too big — they let the tiny bits of salt through.

Q2 Will filtering work for these things?

Write "*Can be filtered out*" or "*Can't be filtered out*" under each picture.

Sugar in Tea

Powdered Coffee

Salt in Soup

....

....

Mystic Margaret's always STIRRING up trouble...

Wow — I bet you never knew there was so much going on when you put some salt in your soup. Just don't start getting the filter paper out at the dinner table — your mum will go up the wall.

Solids in Solutions

Filter paper has very small holes in it, so some things can get through it and some things can't. You can test which things can be filtered by doing an experiment.

Q1 Sinbad wants to get the salt out of his tears, because they're too salty.

I don't reckon filtering will work, but he's going to try it anyway.

a) Write an experiment that Sinbad could do to filter his salty tears.

....

....

....

b) Which four of these things would he need for the experiment?

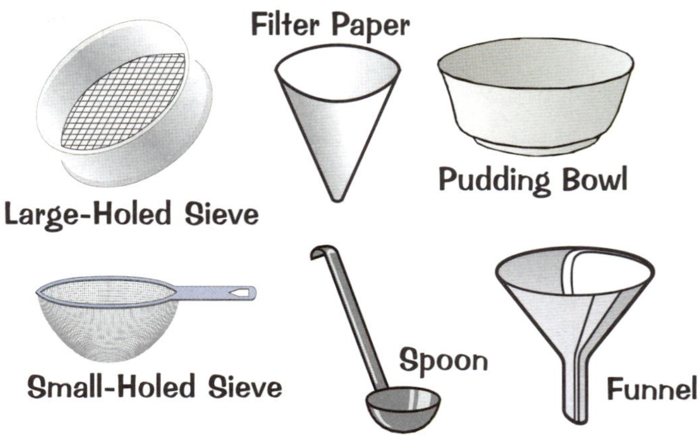

1 ....

2 ....

3 ....

4 ....

Sinbad's tears are too salty for him.

Q2 Sinbad wants to know if all the salt has been filtered out.

Be careful — check with an adult that it's safe before you try tasting anything.

a) Which is the best way to find out?

....

Weighing it. Looking at it. Tasting it. Dipping your finger in it.

b) Will there be any salt left in the water? ....

Filtering salt water — it'll end in tears...

Poor old Sinbad.

Solids in Solutions

You've got to make sure everything is completely clean before you taste anything. That means washing your hands and all your equipment — and using brand new salt and sugar.

Q1 Which of these things must you do before tasting a solution?

Use clean equipment.

Wash your hands.

Wipe your feet.

Use fresh salt or sugar.

Take a deep breath and hope for the best.

Have a lie down.

Write your answers here.

....

....

....

Make sure you wash your hands.

A filter is like a sieve with very small holes. Only really really small bits can fall through it. If something can't be filtered out, it means that the bits are smaller than the holes in the filter.

Q2 These sentences explain why salt and sugar can't be filtered out of a solution. Fill in the gaps using the words in the splodge underneath.

Filters are like .... with very .... holes.

You can't use a .... to get the salt out of salty water because

the filter's holes are .... enough for the bits of salt to get through.

That is why filtered salt water tastes .... — the salt is still in the water.

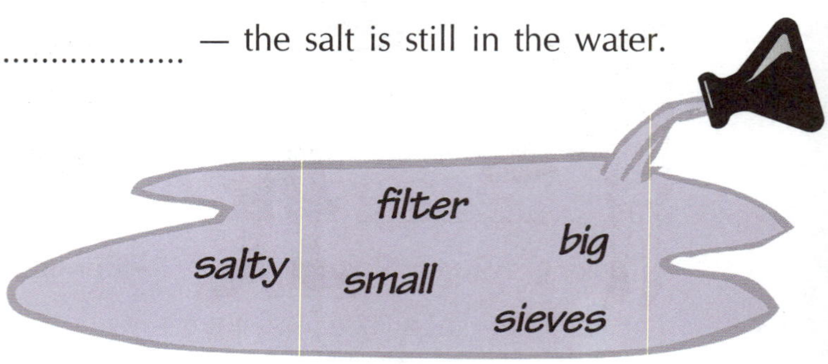

Solutions — I've washed my hands of them...

It's weird — filter paper's got loads of holes in it. Dissolved salt and sugar can get through it, but you can't even see through it. Bit freaky if you ask me...

Solids in Solutions

Q1 Draw the missing bits of each experiment in the spaces provided. For each experiment, say whether the solid has been filtered out or is still in the solution — tick the box next to the right answer.

A

Making a Salt Solution

Filtering the Solution

Tasting the Solution

The salt has a) stayed in the solution. ☐

b) been filtered out. ☐

B

Making a Coffee Solution

Filtering the Solution

Tasting the Solution

The coffee has a) stayed in the solution. ☐

b) been filtered out. ☐

C

Making a Sugar Solution

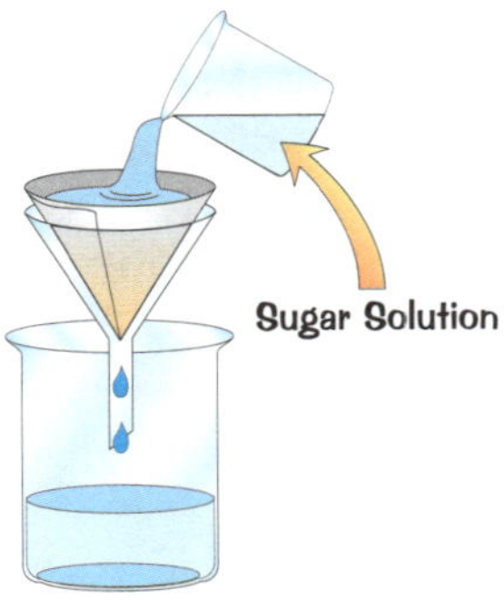

Filtering the Solution

Tasting the Solution

The sugar has a) stayed in the solution. ☐

b) been filtered out. ☐

And now for the taste test...

You can do this yourself, in class or at home. Do all these experiments and then try using different things. But watch out — only use stuff that's OK to taste at the end of the experiment.

Revision Questions

These two pages are where you find out if anything about solids and liquids has stuck in that head of yours. There isn't anything here that you haven't done already — so you've got no excuses.

Q1 The pictures below show a load of solids and liquids.
Put a circle around the name of each thing that's a solid.

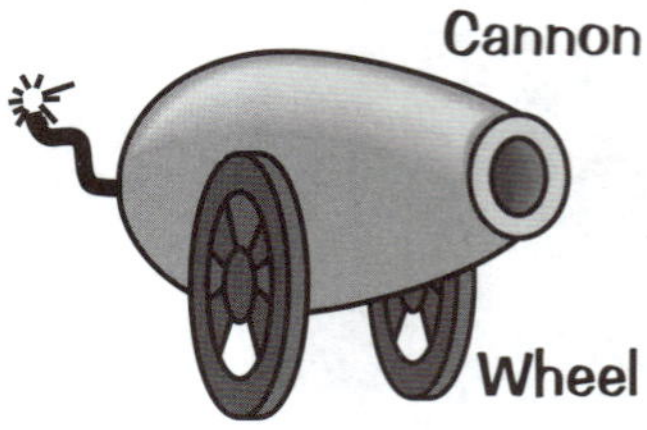

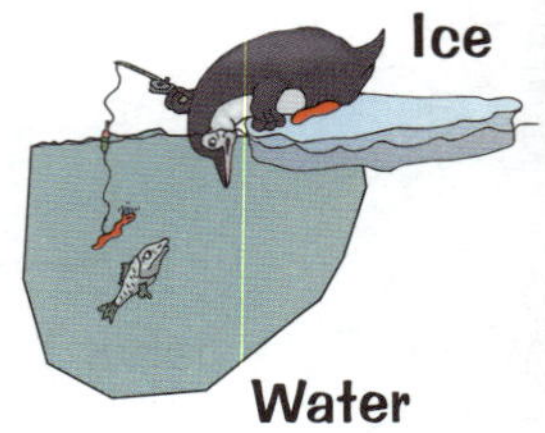

Q2 Make a list of all the liquids named in the pictures above.

Q3 Put a circle around the name of the runniest liquid.

....

....

....

Q4 There are three different measuring bottles below.

Draw the right amount of the liquid in each bottle, and colour in the liquid.

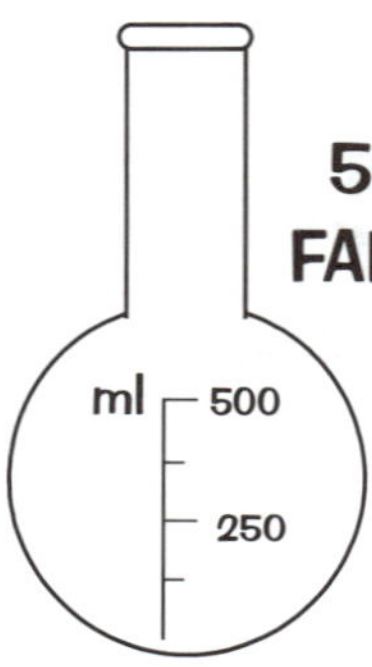

500 ml of FAKE BLOOD

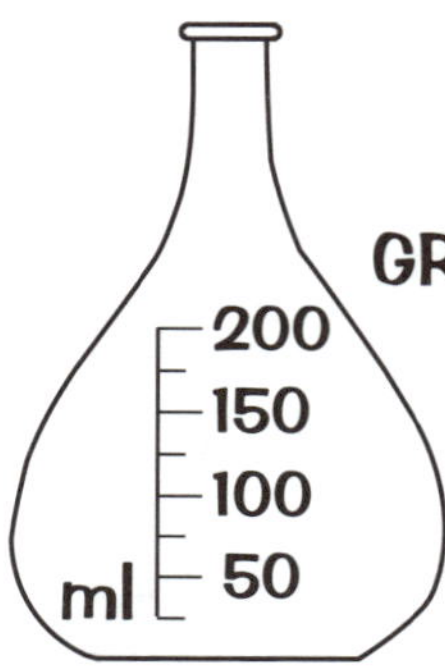

150 ml of GREEN GUNGE

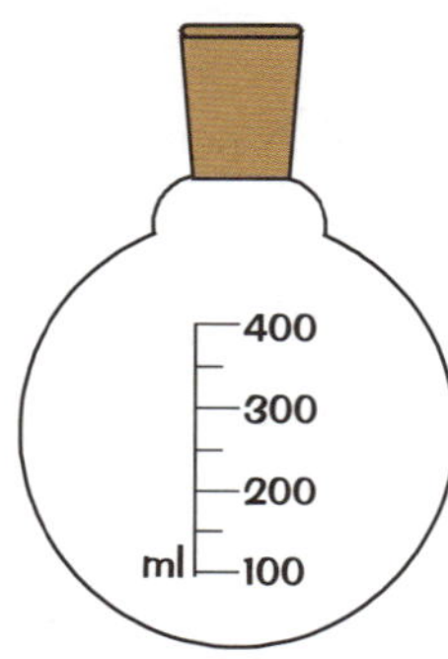

100 ml of BLUE SHAMPOO

Q5 Put a tick next to each of the solids below which acts like a liquid.

TV ☐

Flour ☐

Window ☐

Sand ☐

Q6 Why do some solids act like liquids? (Tick the right answer.)

Because they're made up of tiny little bits. ☐

Because they're really light. ☐

Act like a liquid? — I'd rather act like DiCaprio...

OK, time to whizz through these pages. You've done it all before, so it should be easy enough. If you do get stuck, don't panic, just look back in the book to whatever you're stuck on.

Revision Questions

Q1 Sam's got to separate rice from water. Put a tick next to the thing that she should use.

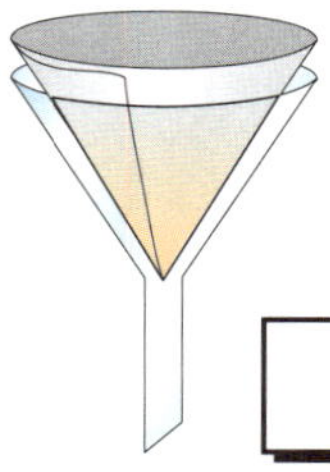
Filter paper in funnel ☐

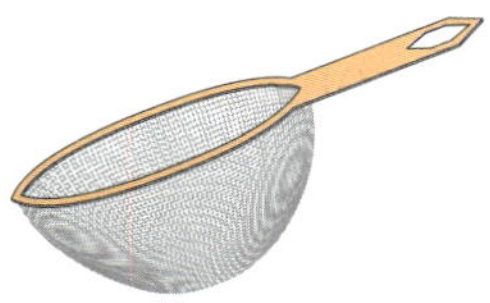
Small-holed sieve ☐

Fishing net ☐

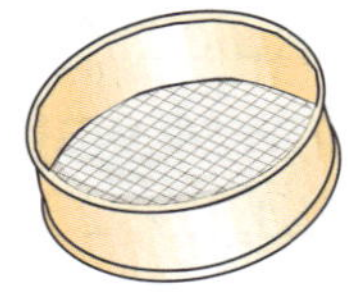
Large-holed sieve ☐

Q2 Why wouldn't she use the fishing net? ....

Q3 Which one of the objects above would you use to separate golf balls from rice? ....

Q4 Fill in the gaps in the sentences below using words from the snowman.

If you have some ice and you put it in a warm oven, it will turn into a .... When ice turns into water, that's called .... When you have some water and you make it really ...., it will become solid. It has turned into .... This is called ....

Q5 I want to know what will happen to each of these solids when I put them in water. Write under each one whether it will <u>dissolve</u>, <u>not dissolve</u> or <u>react</u>.

rice

....

sugar

....

sand

....

plaster of Paris

....

Q6 Can you use a filter to take the salt out of a salt water solution? (Yes or no.) ....

Q7 If you filtered a salt water solution, would the water taste salty afterwards? ....

That's all, folks...

That's it. The end of the book. Well, apart from the index, that is. It's quite a good index, as indexes go. Well worth a read. Apart from that, you should be an expert on solids and liquids now.

Index